MY FIRST GUIDE TO SPACE

My FIRST GUIDE TO SPACE

CAMILLA
DE LA BEDOYERE

ILLUSTRATED BY

AARON CUSHLEY

BPP

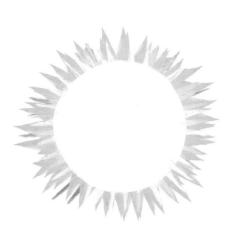

CONTENTS

WHAT IS SPACE?

OUTER SPACE

THE SOLAR SYSTEM

THE SPACE AGE

SHOOTING STAR SEARCH

Can you find the blue shooting stars hiding in this book?
There is one in every scene except one.

Go to page 57 to find out which scene is the exception.

METEOR

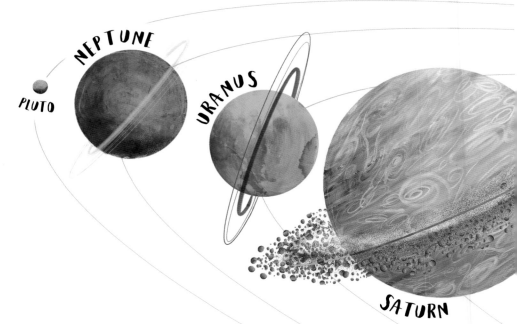
PLUTO
NEPTUNE
URANUS
SATURN

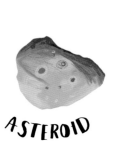
ASTEROID

WHAT IS SPACE?

METEOR SHOWER

SATELLITE

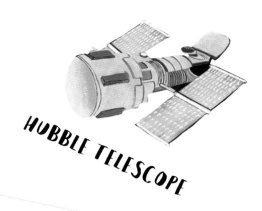

HUBBLE TELESCOPE

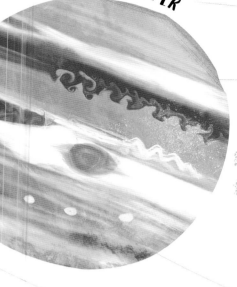

JUPITER

MOON

MARS

VENUS

EARTH

MERCURY

ASTEROID BELT

THE
SUN

THE UNIVERSE

Space is enormous! It starts way above Earth's surface, about 60 miles/100 kilometers up. Planets, stars, asteroids, and comets are just a few examples of what can be found in outer space.

The universe encompasses everything that can be found in space. It was formed about 13.8 billion years ago.

The solar system was formed about 4.5 billion years ago. It is composed of our sun and the planets that orbit it, including Earth, plus other orbiting objects, such as the dwarf planet Pluto.

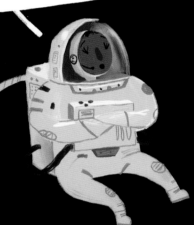

You are made of billions of particles, and all of them were created when the universe first began.

Telescope

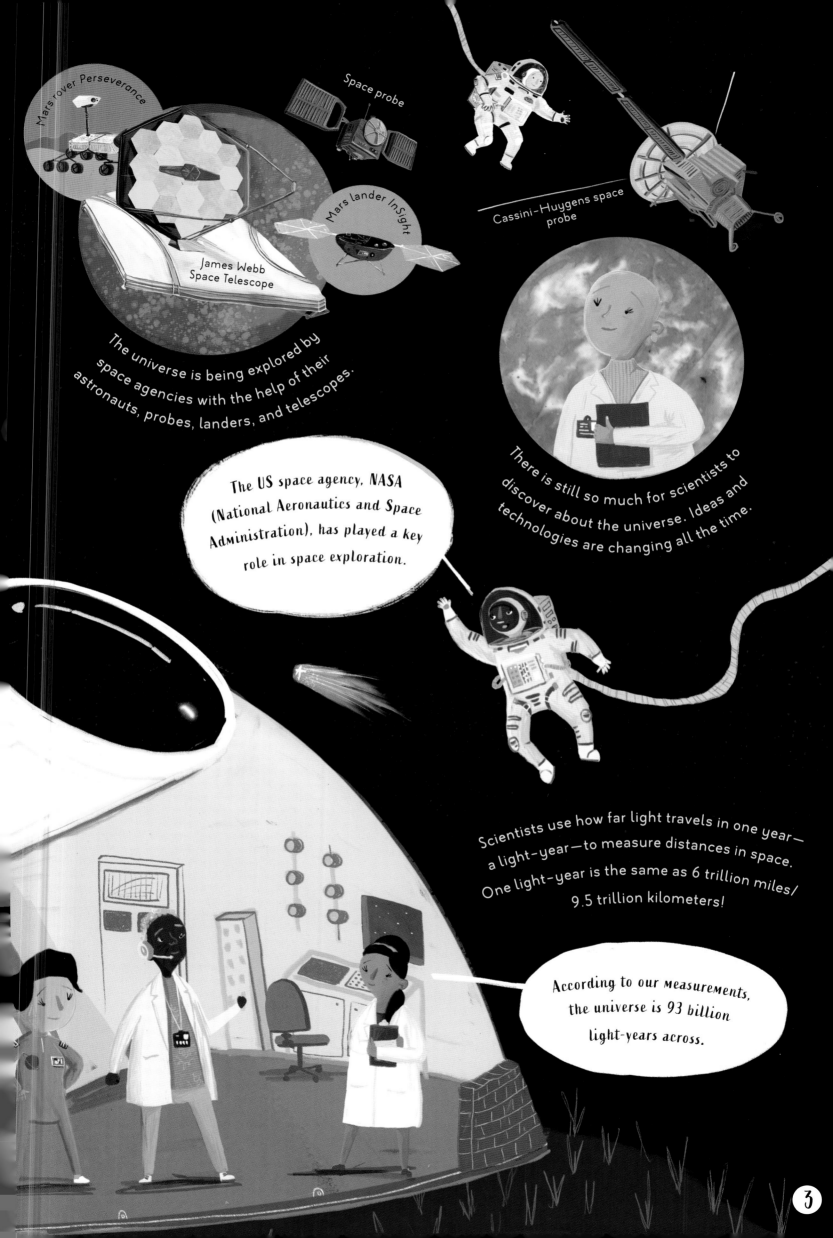

Mars rover Perseverance

Space probe

James Webb Space Telescope

Mars lander InSight

Cassini-Huygens space probe

The universe is being explored by space agencies with the help of their astronauts, probes, landers, and telescopes.

There is still so much for scientists to discover about the universe. Ideas and technologies are changing all the time.

The US space agency, NASA (National Aeronautics and Space Administration), has played a key role in space exploration.

Scientists use how far light travels in one year— a light-year—to measure distances in space. One light-year is the same as 6 trillion miles/ 9.5 trillion kilometers!

According to our measurements, the universe is 93 billion light-years across.

THE BIG BANG

Long ago, everything in the universe was in a tiny space. It then started to stretch and expand into something much, much bigger. That moment is called the Big Bang.

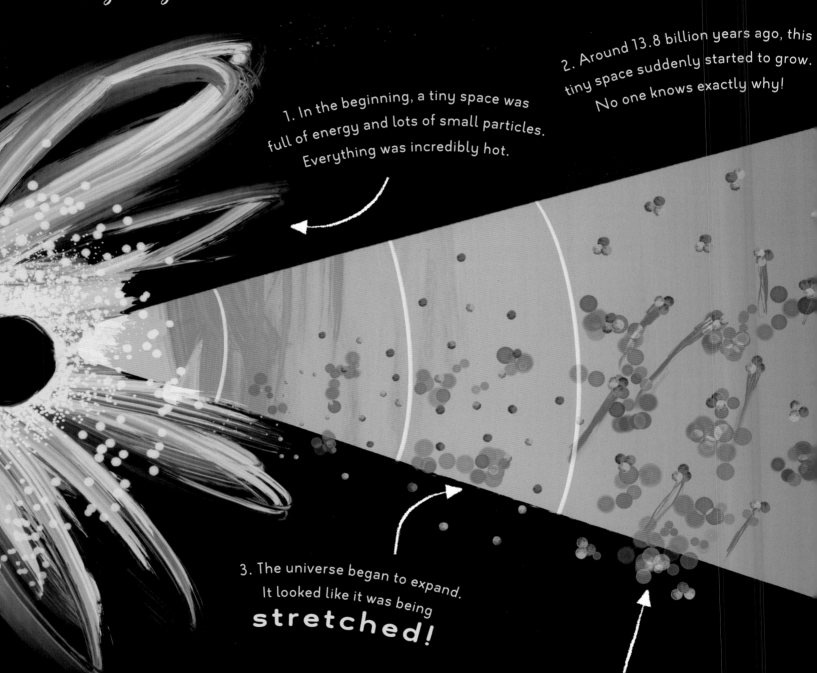

2. Around 13.8 billion years ago, this tiny space suddenly started to grow. No one knows exactly why!

1. In the beginning, a tiny space was full of energy and lots of small particles. Everything was incredibly hot.

3. The universe began to expand. It looked like it was being **stretched!**

4. Then the universe began to cool and tiny particles started to form groups called atoms.

Seconds after the Big Bang, the universe's temperature was 1,830 trillion°F/1,000 trillion°C.

In 1990, a rocket launched the Hubble Space Telescope into space. Hubble helps scientists theorize what may have happened when the universe began.

5. A force called gravity made the atoms clump together. This clumping led to the first stars and galaxies, less than half a billion years after the Big Bang.

6. As stars were born, grew, and died, asteroids, planets, and comets began to form.

THE SOLAR SYSTEM

The solar system consists of the sun and all the objects that travel around it, including eight planets and many moons, asteroids, and meteors.

The solar system formed more than 4 billion years ago, from clouds of dust and gas.

VENUS

The four planets that are closest to the sun are Mercury, Venus, Earth, and Mars. They are solid and mostly made of rock.

A moon orbits a planet. Mercury and Venus are the only planets without moons, but there are more than 250 moons in the solar system, with more being discovered.

THE SUN

EARTH **MOON**

Earth is the biggest rocky planet.

MERCURY

ASTEROID BELT

The planets travel around, or orbit, the sun because they are pulled toward it by the force of gravity. The planets also spin like tops as they travel.

MARS

The path that each planet follows around the sun is called its orbit. A planet's orbit is not a perfect circle. It looks more like an egg shape, or oval.

Jupiter, Saturn, Uranus, and Neptune are huge balls of gas and are known as gas giants.

Jupiter and Saturn are the largest planets in the solar system.

SATURN

JUPITER

NEPTUNE

PLUTO

In 2006, scientists changed Pluto's classification to that of a dwarf planet.

Being far from the sun, Uranus and Neptune are both very cold; they're known as ice giants.

URANUS

The time it takes for a planet to spin once is called a day. A day on Earth lasts 24 hours; a day on Jupiter is almost 10 Earth hours long.

The asteroid belt lies between Mars and Jupiter. This belt contains millions of rocky, icy, or metallic objects orbiting the sun. One of the largest asteroids is named Vesta; it measures 326 miles/525 kilometers across.

The time it takes for a planet to orbit the sun is called a year. A year on Earth lasts about 365 days.

EARTH AND ITS MOON

Our home planet, Earth, is special because it can support life. Seen from space, Earth appears mostly blue because much of it is covered in water.

Earth is about 4.5 billion years old. For a long time, it was a hot, dry, lifeless place that was blasted by asteroids and comets.

N

Earth is slightly tilted on its side. This tilt gives us seasons: spring, summer, fall, and winter.

About 3.8 billion years ago, the oceans formed and the first living things began to appear. As far as we know, Earth is the only place in space where life exists.

Earth's atmosphere traps the sun's heat like a blanket. This means that in general, Earth's temperature is neither too hot nor too cold, but just right for living things.

The atmosphere also contains the air that animals and plants need to survive. And it is where various types of weather, such as wind, rain, and snow, are formed.

S

There are seven large areas of land on Earth's surface called continents. The large areas of salty water are called oceans.

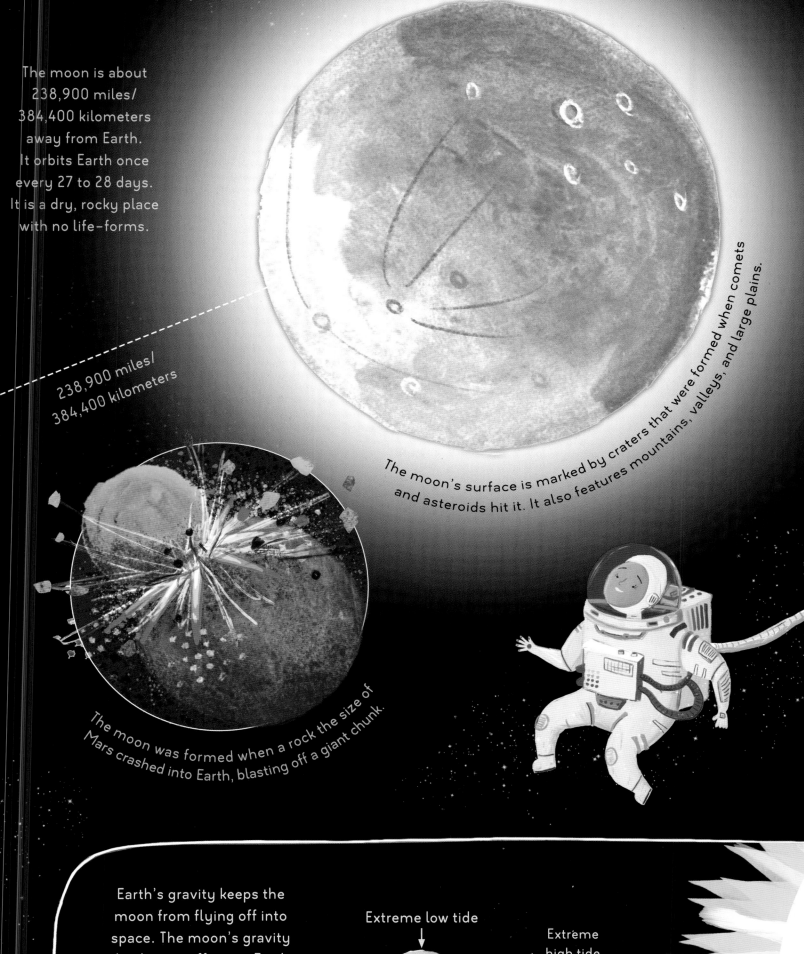

The moon is about 238,900 miles/ 384,400 kilometers away from Earth. It orbits Earth once every 27 to 28 days. It is a dry, rocky place with no life-forms.

238,900 miles/ 384,400 kilometers

The moon's surface is marked by craters that were formed when comets and asteroids hit it. It also features mountains, valleys, and large plains.

The moon was formed when a rock the size of Mars crashed into Earth, blasting off a giant chunk.

Earth's gravity keeps the moon from flying off into space. The moon's gravity also has an effect on Earth. It is not a strong force, but it does affect the oceans, resulting in low and high tides depending on Earth's position in relation to the moon.

Extreme low tide

Extreme high tide

Extreme low tide

THE NIGHT SKY

When we look up into the inky darkness of the night sky, we catch a glimpse of the wonders of the universe. Twinkling stars glow alongside the moon, and rocky visitors from space zoom past on their long-distance travels.

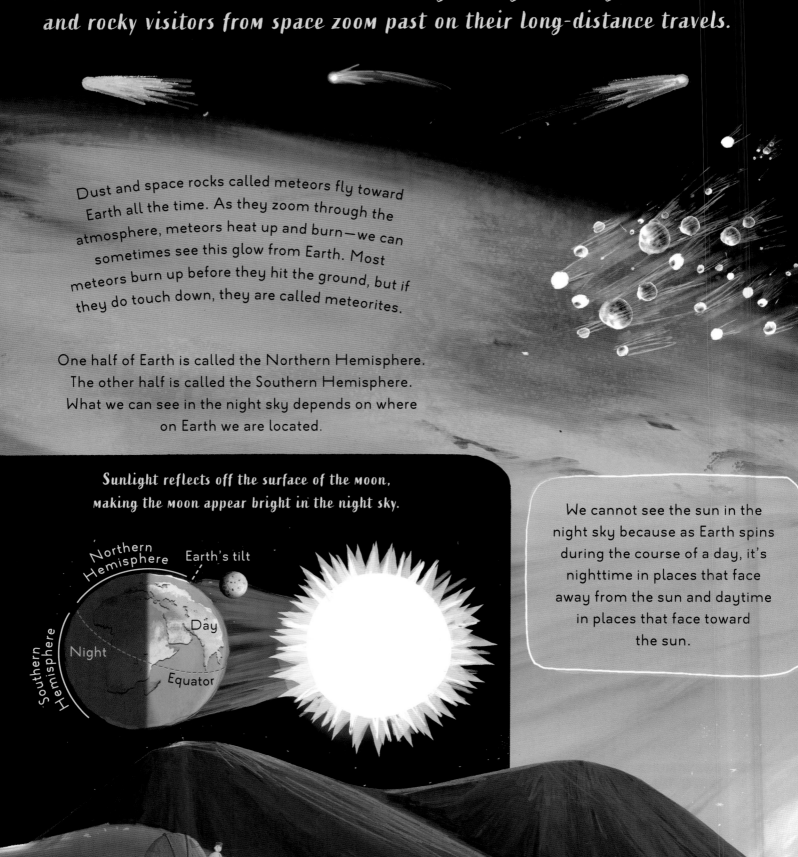

Dust and space rocks called meteors fly toward Earth all the time. As they zoom through the atmosphere, meteors heat up and burn—we can sometimes see this glow from Earth. Most meteors burn up before they hit the ground, but if they do touch down, they are called meteorites.

One half of Earth is called the Northern Hemisphere. The other half is called the Southern Hemisphere. What we can see in the night sky depends on where on Earth we are located.

Sunlight reflects off the surface of the moon, making the moon appear bright in the night sky.

Northern Hemisphere

Earth's tilt

Southern Hemisphere

Night

Day

Equator

We cannot see the sun in the night sky because as Earth spins during the course of a day, it's nighttime in places that face away from the sun and daytime in places that face toward the sun.

THIRD QUARTER

WANING CRESCENT

WANING GIBBOUS

Cassiopeia is a group of five bright stars that, if connected by imaginary lines, could make a letter W.

NEW MOON

FULL MOON

There are eight phases of the moon.

On a clear night, we can see the moon in the night sky. Over the course of the moon's month-long orbit, Earth casts its shadow on it from shifting angles, making the moon's circle appear to increase and decrease in what are known as phases.

Some planets can be seen from Earth. Venus is the brightest object in the night sky after the moon, and it can be seen without a telescope.

WAXING CRESCENT

WAXING GIBBOUS

FIRST QUARTER

The largest artificial satellite that orbits Earth is the International Space Station, where scientists work for months at a time.

Satellites are machines sent into space to help with research, track Earth's weather, and transmit messages. They can also measure the size of forests and the temperature of the oceans.

morning, the sun appears to rise in the east. At the end of day, it seems to disappear below the horizon in the west.

ASTRONOMY

Astronomers study space to find out more about the galaxies, stars, planets, and comets.

Modern astronomers use special equipment, from simple binoculars to huge telescopes on mountains or in deserts. Space telescopes have even been sent beyond Earth's atmosphere to explore and observe objects far from Earth.

A giant telescope in the Atacama Desert, in South America, is one of the largest and highest telescopes on Earth. It has very sensitive cameras and can detect new stars, black holes, and energy left over from the Big Bang.

As the Hubble Space Telescope orbits Earth, it takes pictures of distant stars, planets, and galaxies. It is able to view objects more than 13 billion light-years away from Earth.

An observatory is a special building where astronomers use telescopes and other equipment to look at and study space.

The first light telescope was invented more than 400 years ago. These simple telescopes are tube shaped, and their lenses can magnify images from far away. Modern telescopes also use light to see into space and can also detect different types of energy that we can't see, such as radio waves.

The first astronomers used math to study the stars—they calculated the size of Earth and its distance from the sun, without the use of telescopes.

Astronomers in ancient Greece, Babylonia (now Iraq), and China followed star movements in the sky to devise calendars and created sky maps to show star positions throughout the year.

Astronomers of the ancient Mayan civilization (in modern-day southern Mexico and northern Central America) tracked and predicted solar eclipses. A solar eclipse occurs when the moon passes between Earth and the sun, blocking out light and turning the sky dark for a few minutes.

SUPERNOVA

THE
SUN

OUTER
SPACE

RED GIANT

SPIRAL GALAXY

NEUTRON STAR

ASTEROID

BLACK HOLE

RED SUPERGIANT

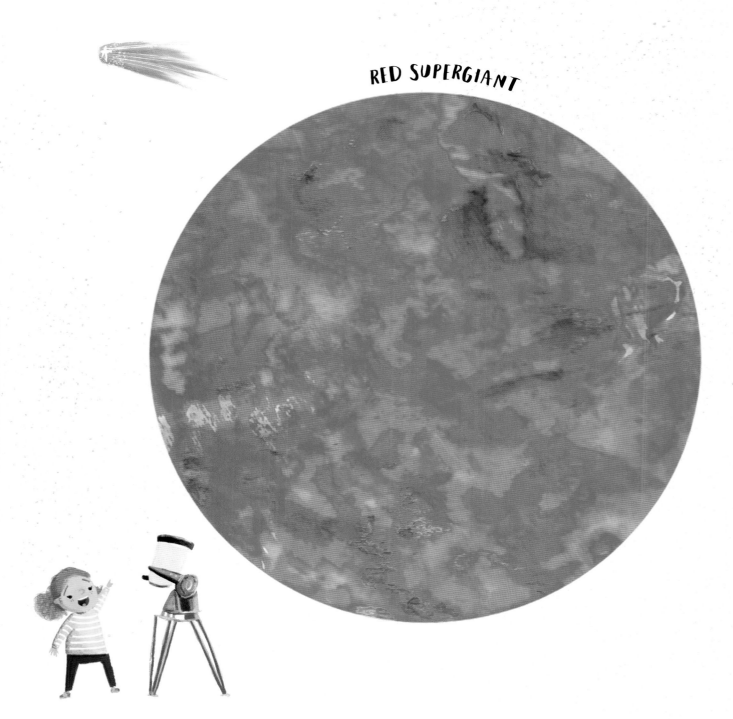

THE LIFE OF A STAR

A star is born when gas and dust are pulled together by gravity. Some stars glow for billions of years, but as they get older, they change and eventually die.

Start here!

MASSIVE STAR

A star begins with a cloud of gas and dust called a nebula.

NEBULA

Gravity pulls the dust and gas into the nebula's center. When it gets too heavy, the nebula collapses and becomes what's called a protostar. It gets hotter and hotter until it becomes a star. Stars shine because they release huge amounts of light energy.

PROTOSTAR

HIGH-MASS STAR

Massive stars live for only a few million years before they expand and become supergiant stars, which are usually red or blue and shine very brightly.

AVERAGE-MASS STAR

The amount of material that makes up an object is called its mass. Some stars have a high mass, but most have either an average mass or a low mass.

LOW-MASS STAR

RED DWARF

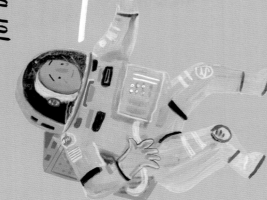

Red dwarf stars are the most common type of stars. They live much longer than high-mass stars because they use up their fuel—hydrogen and helium gases—more slowly.

RED SUPERGIANT

A supergiant star uses up its fuel quickly and ends its short life in an enormous explosion called a supernova. It shines more brightly than a whole galaxy of stars and collapses, becoming a neutron star or a black hole.

Dust and gas can speed away from an exploding supernova at more than 6,000 miles/10,000 kilometers a second!

BLACK HOLE

The stars with the greatest mass collapse into a black hole, where gravity is so strong even light cannot escape.

SUPERNOVA

NEUTRON STAR

A neutron star is small, but it still has the same mass as a much larger star. This makes it spin very fast.

SUN-LIKE STAR

Our sun is about five billion years old. It will live for a total of about 10 billion years, glowing with heat and light.

RED GIANT

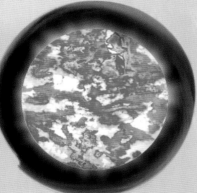

Near the end of its life, a sun-like star begins to run out of fuel and gets hotter and bigger. It turns into a red giant star.

PLANETARY NEBULA

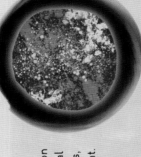

As the red giant dies, it begins to shed its outer layers, creating an expanding cloud of gas. This is called a planetary nebula. What's left of the former star's core transforms into a white dwarf.

Red dwarf stars live for trillions of years, then **slowly fade away and become white dwarfs.**

WHITE DWARF

With its fuel used up, a red dwarf collapses and shrinks, becoming a white dwarf. Or, once the outer layers of a planetary nebula dissipate, it reveals a white dwarf.

BLACK DWARF

When a white dwarf cools, it becomes a black dwarf. This takes so long that the universe is too young to have any black dwarfs yet!

THE SUN

The sun is a star, a huge ball of glowing gas that gives off lots of energy, such as heat and light. Without a telescope, we can see about 6,000 stars in the night sky, but there are trillions more.

The sun is the nearest star to Earth, and without it, there would be no life. It's almost five billion years old and so big that 1.3 million Earths would fit inside it.

Sunlight travels at 186,000 miles/300,000 kilometers a second, which means it takes eight minutes and 20 seconds to reach Earth.

The sun also makes other types of energy, such as X-ray radiation and ultraviolet radiation. Radiation can be harmful, which is why we protect our skin and eyes in strong sunlight.

The sun is 93 million miles/150 million kilometers from Earth. It's packed with superheated hydrogen and helium gases that glow at 10,000°F/5,500°C at the surface.

The surface of the sun is called the photosphere. It is made of a superhot mixture of gases called plasma, which is always moving.

The sun is the biggest object in the solar system.

At its center, the sun's heat rockets to an incredible 27 million°F/15 million°C!

The sun's atmosphere includes a thin layer of gases called the chromosphere. Beyond that is an outer layer called the corona, which creates a solar wind that spreads millions of miles into space.

The word corona means crown. The sun's corona looks like a crown because jets of hot gas shoot out of it. They are called solar flares.

GALAXIES

A galaxy is an enormous group of stars, planets, gas, and dust. Our galaxy is called the Milky Way, and on a clear night, you can see it without using a telescope.

There are three main types of galaxies: spiral, elliptical, and irregular. They are all different shapes and sizes.

SPIRAL GALAXY
Spiral galaxies are flat, like a disk, and have long spiral arms.

ELLIPTICAL GALAXY
Elliptical galaxies are shaped like ovals, with lots of stars near the center.

IRREGULAR GALAXY
Irregular galaxies resemble starry blobs. They form when other galaxies crash into each other.

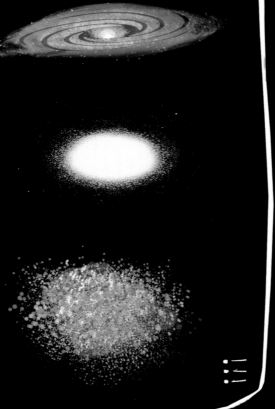

THE MILKY WAY

The Milky Way has a black hole called Sagittarius A* at its center.

The Milky Way is a spiral galaxy. Everything in the Milky Way, including the solar system, travels around its center.

The solar system takes about 250 million years to travel around the Milky Way.

The spiral galaxy Andromeda is the closest galaxy to the Milky Way, but it is bigger, with twice as many stars. Andromeda has multiple black holes—places in space where gravity sucks everything in, even light.

ANDROMEDA

There are billions of galaxies in the universe. The largest galaxies contain trillions of stars.

Andromeda can be seen with the naked eye, even though it is 2.5 million light-years away.

STARGAZING IN THE NORTH

Some stars appear to make patterns in the sky called constellations. Thirty-six of the 88 constellations recognized by the International Astronomical Union can be seen from the Northern Hemisphere.

Many constellations are named for the mythical characters or animals that people thought the star groupings resembled.

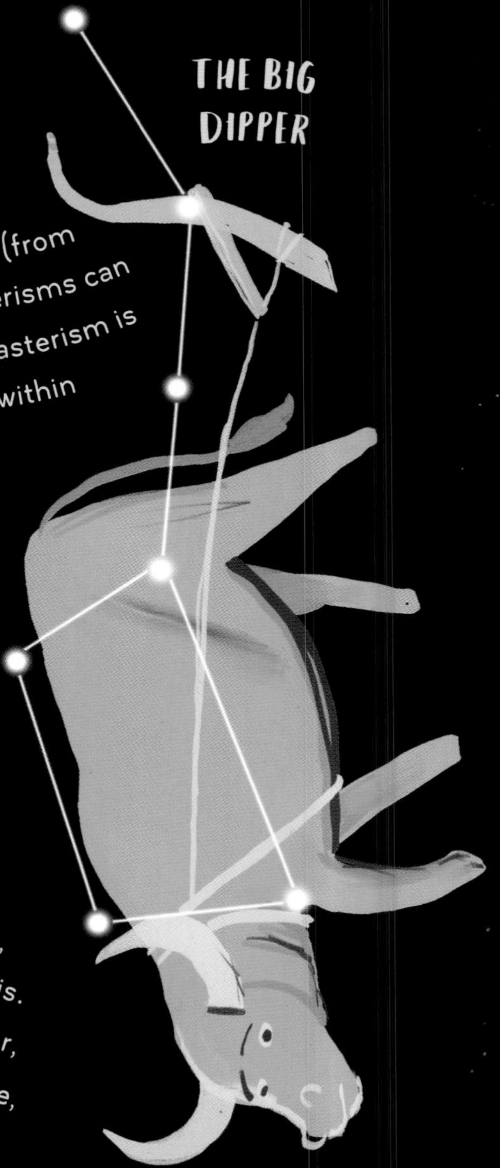

A pattern of stars is called an asterism (from the Greek word *aster*, meaning star). Asterisms can be part of a constellation. The Big Dipper asterism is also known as the Plow and is found within the constellation Ursa Major.

THE BIG DIPPER

Ursa Minor, or the Little Bear constellation, contains one of the most famous stars: Polaris. This bright star is also known as the North Star, or the polestar. It appears above the North Pole, so you can use it like a compass.

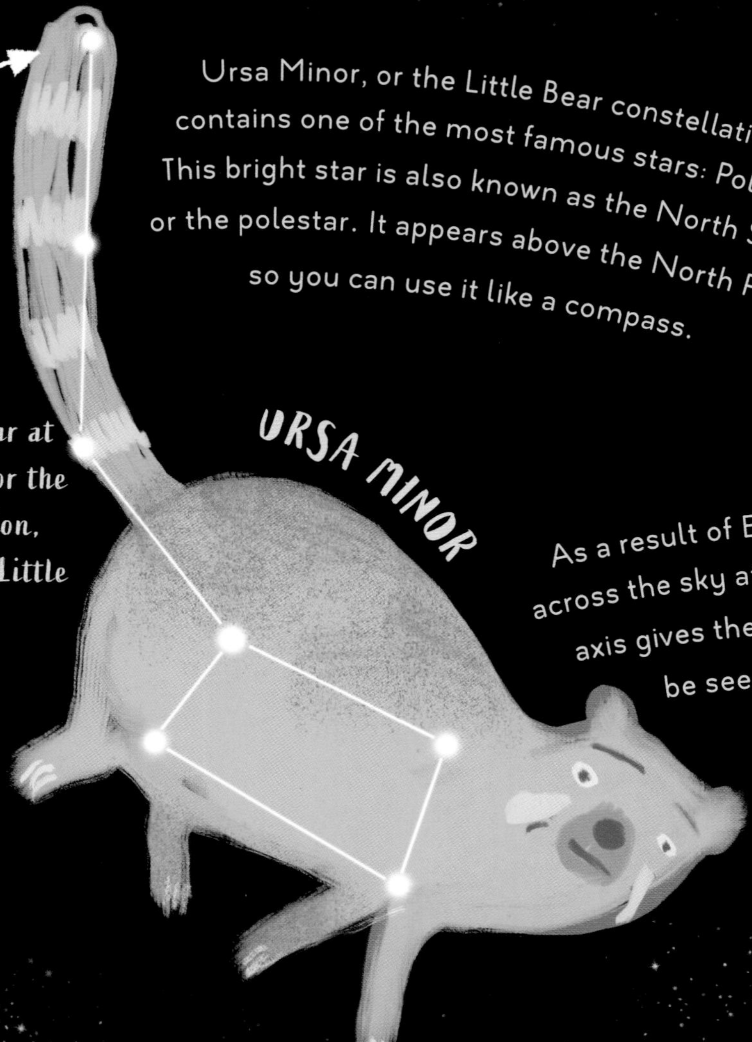

Polaris is the bright star at one end of Ursa Minor, or the Little Bear constellation, which is also called the Little Dipper.

URSA MINOR

As a result of Earth's orbit, constellations appear to m across the sky at night. Polaris's position at Earth's nort axis gives the impression that it doesn't move. It can be seen from the Southern Hemisphere.

URSA MAJOR

There are 20 main stars in Ursa Major, or the Great Bear constellation, and 135 in total. It is one of the largest constellations.

The constellation Leo looks like a lion. The brightest star is called Regulus, although it is actually a grouping of four stars. The best time to see Regulus is in winter or spring.

Including Regulus, there are 14 named stars in the constellation Leo, some of which are paired.

LEO

REGULUS

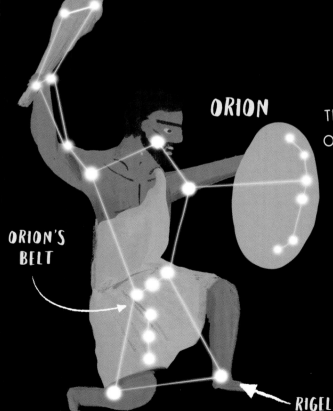

ORION

ORION'S BELT

RIGEL

The constellation Orion is also called the Hunter. Orion's Belt is made up of three bright stars, and one of the Hunter's feet is a supergiant star named Rigel.

When you look for Orion in the Northern Hemisphere, you will always find it in the southern part of the sky.

STARGAZING IN THE SOUTH

Stargazers see different constellations in the night sky, depending on where they are and the time of year. In the Southern Hemisphere, there are some constellations that are rarely, or never, seen in the north, while some are seen in both hemispheres but from different perspectives.

Fifty-two of the 88 constellations recognized by the International Astronomical Union can be seen in the Southern Hemisphere.

CRUX

Crux is the smallest constellation. It is also referred to as the Southern Cross, which is an asterism of four bright stars and a fifth fainter star. It can be used to help locate the South Pole.

The brightest and southernmost star in the Crux constellation is called Acrux. An imaginary line from the northernmost star to Acrux points toward the South Pole.

The constellation Centaurus is named after a centaur, a mythical creature that is half human, half horse. It includ one of the brightest stars in the night sky, Alpha Centauri A which is 4.4 light-years away—that's about 26 trillion miles/42 trillion kilometers!

Centaurus is the ninth-largest constellation.

CENTAURUS

Alpha Centauri is the star closest to the solar system and is seen best in the Southern Hemisphere.

The stars in the constellation Scorpius create a shape that looks like a scorpion. It can sometimes be seen in the Northern Hemisphere in summer, near the horizon.

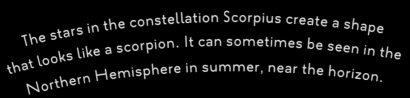

SCORPIUS

Antares is a red supergiant star and the brightest star in Scorpius. It appears orange and is about 550 light-years from Earth.

In Greek mythology, Scorpius is sent to kill Orion, the hunter, but can never catch him. Scorpius rises in the east only after the constellation Orion has set in the west.

Shaula is the second-brightest star in Scorpius. It is actually a cluster of stars and makes up part of the scorpion's raised tail.

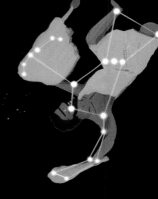

Orion can be seen in both the Northern and Southern Hemispheres, but in the south, it appears upside down!

COMETS

When a giant cosmic snowball swishes past Earth, it gets heated up and glows, creating a startling sight in the sky. This snowball is a comet—just one of many flying visitors from space.

Comets are made of frozen gas, ice, rock, and dust. The largest ones are the size of towns, but the smallest ones are just a few miles wide.

When comets move closer to the the sun, they heat up and the frozen gases in them melt. This creates an enormous glowing cloud called a coma that can be wider than a planet.

The glowing gas and dust form a tail that can be millions of miles long. The tail always stretches away from the sun.

The most famous comet is called Halley's comet, which flies past Earth about once every 76 years. Its next visit will be in 2061.

ASTEROIDS

Asteroids are rocky objects that orbit the sun. Millions of them can be found in the asteroid belt between Mars and Jupiter.

Asteroids are smaller than planets.

Many asteroids measure about a half a mile/ one kilometer or more in diameter— that's almost the length of 10 soccer fields!

In 2021, a mission called the Double Asteroid Redirection Test (DART) sent a spacecraft into outer space to crash into an asteroid called Dimorphos. In 2022, DART successfully impacted Dimorphos's orbit.

Being able to change an asteroid's direction could be helpful if a big asteroid were to head toward Earth.

Around 66 million years ago, a giant asteroid crashed into Earth, starting fires, storms, and volcanic eruptions that pumped toxic gases into the air. Scientists think this event caused the dinosaurs to die out.

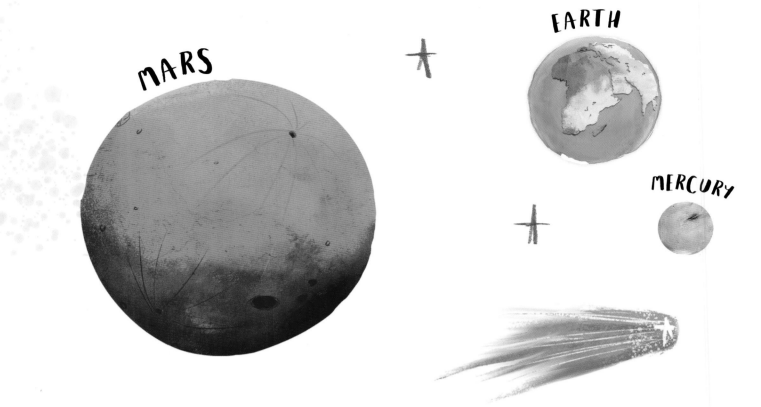

MARS

EARTH

MERCURY

THE SOLAR SYSTEM

VENUS

PLUTO

SATURN

NEPTUNE

JUPITER

URANUS

MERCURY AND VENUS

Mercury is the smallest planet in the solar system and the one closest to the sun. Mercury and Venus are best seen at dawn or dusk, when the sun is below the horizon. After the moon, Venus is the brightest object in the night sky.

Mercury has the shortest year of any planet: it takes just 88 Earth days to orbit the sun. That means an eight-year-old earthling would have celebrated 33 birthdays on Mercury!

Mercury is the fastest planet in the solar system, zooming around the sun at 29 miles/47 kilometers a second.

The Caloris Basin measures almost 1,000 miles/1,600 kilometers across, making it the largest crater on Mercury and one of the largest craters in the solar system.

The surface of Mercury is dry, rocky, and splattered with huge craters, just like our moon.

Mercury has no moons and almost no atmosphere.

Mercury is so close to the sun that it can reach a blistering 800°F/430°C in the day, which is hot enough to melt metal. At night the temperature drops to −290°F/−180°C.

Long ago, Venus may have been covered in oceans, just like Earth. The oceans disappeared with the planet's increasing heat, and volcanoes released toxic gases, forming thick clouds.

Venus is wrapped in a thick blanket of gases, making it even hotter than Mercury.

There are thousands of volcanoes on Venus, and at least 167 of them are bigger than the largest volcano on Earth.

Space probes have flown beneath Venus's clouds to get a better view. Some of the probes have been crushed by the planet's atmosphere or burned up in its heat.

The air on Venus is much denser than on Earth. In fact, it's so heavy that a puff of wind wouldn't cool you down, but it could knock you over!

Venus has long days because it spins very slowly, taking 243 Earth days to spin once. It also spins in the opposite direction from the other planets.

The wind on Venus can whoosh across the surface faster than any winds on Earth— up to 220 miles/360 kilometers per hour.

MARS

Mars, named after the Roman god of war, appears as a bright-red dot in the sky, making it easy to find on a clear night. It is often called the Red Planet.

Mars has two potato-shaped moons: Phobos and Deimos. In 50 million years, Phobos will crash into Mars and create a ring of spinning rocks and dust.

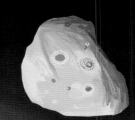

N

A day on Mars is called a sol, which is short for "solar day." One sol lasts about the same time as a day on Earth, but a year lasts 687 Earth days. Like Earth, Mars has seasons.

Valles Marineris is a system of canyons that extends 2,500 miles/4,000 kilometers along the surface of Mars.

Mars is half the size of Earth.

S

Mars has a north pole and south pole, which are cold and icy. The ice on Mars is made of carbon dioxide and water.

Mars is home to the largest mountain in the solar system, Olympus Mons, which is almost 16 miles/25 kilometers high, making it 2.5 times taller than Mauna Loa, the tallest volcano on Earth.

Enormous dust clouds and red sandstorms are whipped up by the wind.

Olympus Mons is a volcano that has been dormant, or inactive, for 25 million years.

It would take astronauts about seven months to get to Mars. On arrival, they would find a freezing cold, red desert under a pink sky. The planet's surface is peppered with volcanoes, huge plains, deep canyons, and enormous sand dunes.

Billions of years ago, Mars was warmer and wetter and had a thicker atmosphere than it does today. There are signs that there may still be some liquid water hidden under the planet's surface.

Astronauts haven't landed on Mars yet, but any future Martian astronauts would need to wear special space suits to protect them from the planet's harsh conditions.

JUPITER

Jupiter is an enormous gas giant. It has 95 moons and colorful stripes that swirl and speed across its surface.

Jupiter is 2.5 times heavier than all the other planets in the solar system put together! That's why it is named after the king of the Roman gods. Some of its moons are named after Jupiter's children.

Io

EUROPA

GANYMEDE

If Ganymede orbited the sun instead of Jupiter, it would be categorized as a planet rather than a moon.

The four largest moons of Jupiter are Io, Europa, Ganymede, and Callisto. Io is covered in volcanoes. Europa has lots of ice on its surface and oceans of liquid water below. Ganymede is the largest moon in the solar system—bigger than Mercury! The surface of Callisto is covered in ice and craters.

CALLISTO

Jupiter may be mostly gas, but you couldn't fly a spacecraft through it and come out the other side. It's extremely hot, and the weight of the gas pushing down on you would squash your spacecraft.

ABORT MISSION!

The colors on Jupiter's surface are caused by cold, windy clouds of gas.

There are very faint rings around Jupiter. They are made of dust.

The Great Red Spot is a storm that has been raging for hundreds of years. It is bigger than Earth!

A day on Jupiter is shorter than anywhere else in the solar system, lasting just under 10 Earth hours. A year is nearly 12 Earth years long.

Jupiter's "pearls" are storms that spin counterclockwise and appear as white ovals on the planet's southern hemisphere.

SATURN

Saturn is a huge spinning ball of gas surrounded by beautiful rings made of ice. Colorful clouds float above the planet's surface, making it appear many shades of gold, brown, yellow, and gray.

It takes four years for spacecraft to reach Saturn.

The Great White Spot is a giant storm that appears on Saturn's surface once every 30 Earth years.

Saturn's winds can reach speeds of 1,100 miles/1,800 kilometers per hour.

Saturn's seven groups of sparkling rings of ice shimmer in the sun's light. The pieces of ice vary in size, from flecks of dust to mountain-sized boulders.

Saturn spins fast—at more than 22,900 miles/ 36,800 kilometers an hour. A Saturn day lasts just 11 Earth hours.

Saturn's surface is made of swirling gases, with liquid gases below.

It takes 29 Earth years for Saturn to orbit the sun.

TITAN

ENCELADUS

Saturn has more than 146 moons, including Enceladus and Titan. Titan, Saturn's largest moon, has a thick orange atmosphere, which blocks out much of the sunlight.

Enceladus's surface is covered in ice and features fountains of icy crystals.

URANUS AND NEPTUNE

Uranus and Neptune are the mysterious ice giants of the solar system because they are so far away. Neptune is not visible from Earth without a telescope, and Uranus can be seen only occasionally. In fact, Uranus wasn't discovered until 1781 and Neptune in 1846.

Uranus is made up mostly of icy materials that move like a liquid around a small, rocky core. It is tilted so far over that it spins on its side.

Uranus also spins clockwise, like Venus.

Uranus has at least 27 moons, including Titania, Miranda, and Ariel, which are named after characters from William Shakespeare's plays and Alexander Pope's poems.

URANUS

TITANIA

ARIEL

MIRANDA

The atmosphere on Uranus absorbs red light, making the planet appear blue-green.

Uranus is the third-largest planet in the solar system. It has at least 13 rings.

Uranus's inner rings are dark and narrow, while the outer ones are brightly colored.

It takes a long time for Uranus to journey around the sun. One year on Uranus lasts 84 Earth years— or 30,687 Earth days!

Neptune is so far from the sun that we know very little about it. It's a cold, dark planet, with freezing windstorms racing across its surface.

EARTH

Neptune is four times larger than Earth.

NEPTUNE

It has 14 moons and five faint rings circling it.

Neptune appears blue.

One year on Neptune lasts about 165 Earth years and one day lasts 16 Earth hours.

BEYOND THE PLANETS

The solar system does not end at Neptune. It stretches out far into space. Astronomers have found many other objects there that orbit the sun, including dwarf planets such as Pluto.

About a hundred years ago, astronomers guessed there was something else beyond Neptune—they called the mystery object Planet X. In 1930, they finally discovered a planet-like object and named it Pluto.

Pluto has five moons. Charon, the largest moon, is half the size of Pluto. The other moons are Styx, Nix, Kerberos, and Hydra.

Some scientists theorize that Pluto and its moons may have been created when a meteorite smashed into it.

Astronomers expected Pluto to be another gas giant planet. Instead, it's small, rocky, and covered in ice. Now scientists categorize Pluto as a dwarf planet.

There are five dwarf planets: Pluto, Eris, Haumea, Makemake, and Ceres.

ERIS

HAUMEA

MAKEMAKE

CERES

Ceres's surface is full of craters.

Eris is the heaviest dwarf planet.

Haumea is shaped like a potato.

It takes Makemake 305 Earth years to orbit the sun.

PLUTO

The Kuiper Belt is an area beyond Neptune where millions of rocky objects orbit the sun. All the dwarf planets are located here, except for Ceres, which is found in the asteroid belt.

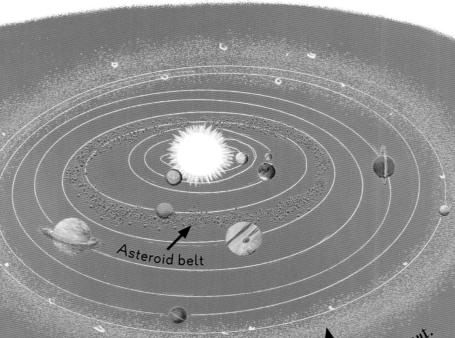

Asteroid belt

The Kuiper Belt is shaped like a doughnut.

Kuiper Belt

Oort Cloud

The Oort Cloud lies beyond the Kuiper Belt. We know very little about it because it would take a spacecraft 300 years to get there.

The Oort Cloud probably contains trillions of icy objects left over from when the solar system was formed.

ROMAN SPACE TELESCOPE

LAIKA

THE SPACE AGE

TRANSITING
EXOPLANET
SURVEY SATELLITE
(TESS)

SOLAR
ORBITER

NEW HORIZONS
SPACE PROBE

ROCKET

INTERNATIONAL SPACE STATION

EAGLE (APOLLO 11
LUNAR MODULE)

SPUTNIK 2

PERSEVERANCE ROVER

MOON

JAMES WEBB
SPACE TELESCOPE

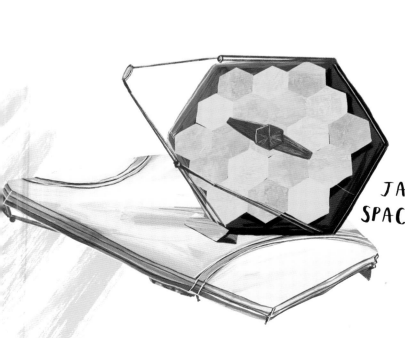

COLUMBIA (APOLLO 11
COMMAND MODULE)

SPACE EXPLORERS

We live in the Space Age—the time in which humans leave Earth to explore beyond. These exciting times need the very best machines that engineers can design and build.

Rockets are powerful machines that carry people and equipment out of Earth's atmosphere and into space.

Rockets carry a payload—an object being taken into space. It could be a space shuttle, satellite, space probe, or people.

We have liftoff!

1. Rocket engines burn fuel. This makes gas, which expands and pushes the rocket up.

2. Extra rockets, called boosters, are also attached to a rocket's side. They fall away when their fuel is used up.

3. A rocket's engine propels the rocket into space.

4. The guidance system makes sure the rocket stays on course and goes where it's supposed to.

5. The payload is carried into space.

Rovers are robot vehicles that explore planets and moons. They can go to places where humans cannot survive. Rovers have wheels so they can move around, picking up samples of rock, taking photographs, and finding out more about the atmosphere.

Landers are spacecraft that can come to rest on the surface of a space object. They have gone to many places, including Venus, a comet, and even Saturn's moon Titan.

Perseverance is a rover that is investigating the Jezero Crater, where scientists think that rivers of water once flowed on Mars.

The *InSight* lander was sent to Mars in 2018 to find out more about the rocks beneath the planet's surface.

Orbiters travel around a space object but do not land on it. The Solar Orbiter is traveling around the sun, finding out more about our star.

The Solar Orbiter is taking the first close-up images of the sun scientists have ever seen.

FIRST JOURNEYS INTO SPACE

The first journeys into space began more than 70 years ago. Since then, many more space missions have taught scientists how humans can survive in space and provided lots of information to help us understand the universe.

Fruit flies were sent into space on board a V2 rocket and returned with the help of a parachute.

1947 The first animals in space were fruit flies. They were sent 60 miles/100 kilometers above Earth. Scientists wanted to know if they would be hurt by going into space, but they returned unharmed.

1957 The first satellite, Sputnik 1, was launched into space. It looked like a small silvery ball and sent radio messages back to Earth.

Gagarin orbited Earth in a capsule. He returned by parachute after a journey that lasted just 108 minutes.

The Vostok 6 rocket took Tereshkova into space. She flew around Earth 48 times.

1961 Yuri Gagarin was the first human to travel into space. He flew on board Vostok 1, orbiting Earth once.

1963 An engineer named Valentina Tereshkova became the first woman in space when she orbited Earth. She is the only woman to travel alone in space so far.

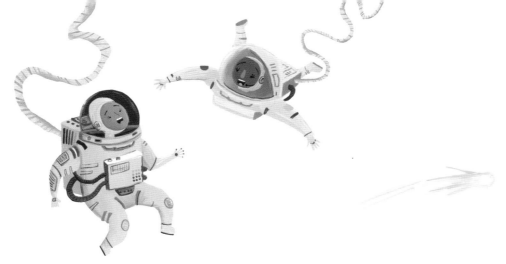

Sputnik 1 was just 23 inches/ 58 centimeters wide. It orbited Earth for three weeks.

Sputnik 1 took about 98 minutes to orbit Earth. It helped scientists learn more about Earth's atmosphere as well as what conditions are like in space.

Laika orbited Earth several times.

1957 Sputnik 2 carried a dog named Laika, who became the first animal to orbit Earth. The mission helped scientists better understand the effects of space flight.

Leonov was attached to the Voskhod 2 spacecraft by a tether so he didn't float away.

1965 Alexei Leonov was the first person to walk— or float—in space! With a backpack containing air to breathe, Leonov spent about 12 minutes outside the spacecraft.

Two space-traveling tortoises flew on the Zond 5 spacecraft.

1968 After a three-day journey, a pair of tortoises became the first living creatures to travel to the moon. The Zond 5 successfully returned to Earth, with images of both Earth and the moon.

WALKING ON THE MOON

On a historic day in 1969, the first humans landed on the moon. In total, the Apollo moon missions took 12 astronauts to the surface of our nearest neighbor.

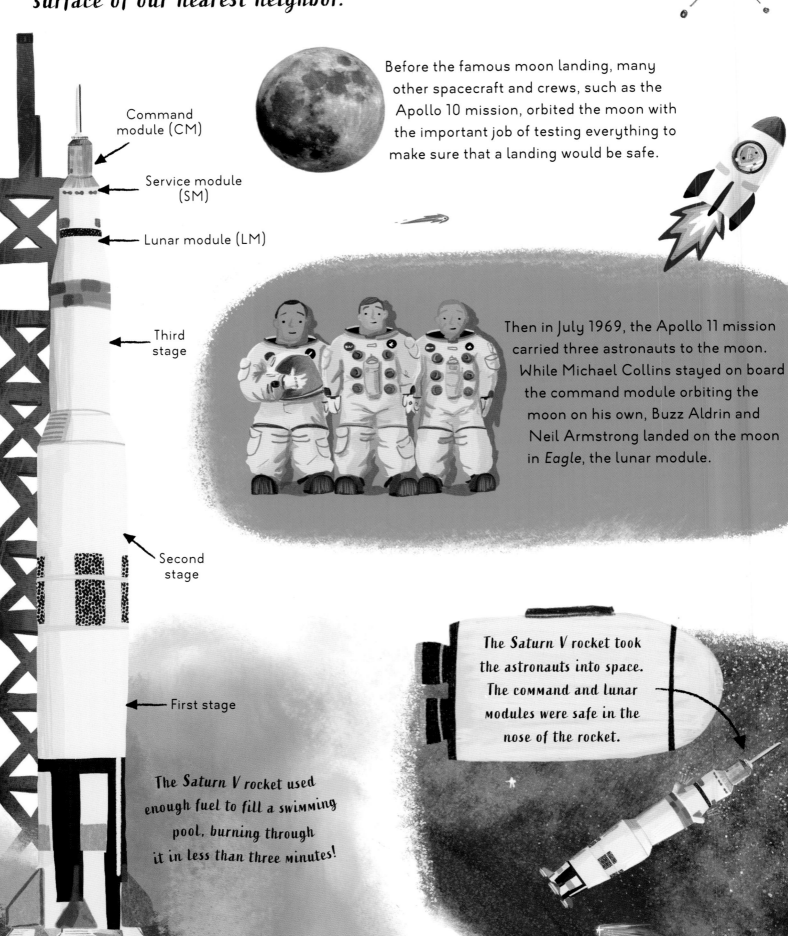

Command module (CM)

Service module (SM)

Lunar module (LM)

Third stage

Second stage

First stage

Before the famous moon landing, many other spacecraft and crews, such as the Apollo 10 mission, orbited the moon with the important job of testing everything to make sure that a landing would be safe.

Then in July 1969, the Apollo 11 mission carried three astronauts to the moon. While Michael Collins stayed on board the command module orbiting the moon on his own, Buzz Aldrin and Neil Armstrong landed on the moon in *Eagle*, the lunar module.

The *Saturn V* rocket took the astronauts into space. The command and lunar modules were safe in the nose of the rocket.

The *Saturn V* rocket used enough fuel to fill a swimming pool, burning through it in less than three minutes!

48

When Eagle safely touched down on a smooth stretch of land called the Sea of Tranquility, it had only 20 seconds' worth of fuel left! Back at base, a mathematician named Katherine Johnson was doing the calculations needed to get the astronauts back again safely.

Johnson was vital to the whole moon landing mission. Her calculations helped get the rocket to the moon, too.

The command module was named *Columbia*.

The lunar module was used for landing on and lifting off from the moon.

After Neil Armstrong took his first steps on the moon's dry and dusty surface, he said, "That's one small step for man, one giant leap for mankind." Back on Earth, more than 600 million people were watching him in awe on television.

The astronauts spent two hours collecting rocks and dust for scientists. Then *Columbia* took the men home, splashing down in the Pacific Ocean.

LIVING IN SPACE

Living in space can be difficult—there is no air, food, or water. With the help of space suits and space stations, astronauts can now survive in space for months at a time.

The International Space Station (ISS) has been in space since 1998. The ISS is a science laboratory that helps scientists better understand space and how humans can live there in the future.

The ISS orbits Earth 16 times a day—once every 93 minutes. It travels at an altitude of 254 miles/408 kilometers and at a speed of 17,200 miles/27,700 kilometers per hour.

The first space station, called Salyut 1, was launched in 1971.

In the ISS science lab, scientists are tracking the effect of low gravity on plants, animals, and humans. They also photograph Earth and monitor the health of oceans and forests.

When astronauts go outside the ISS, they need to be tethered (attached) to the spacecraft and wear space suits. They are able to speak to and hear one another via microphones and speakers in their helmets.

Solar panels on the ISS turn the sun's energy into power, such as electricity.

Space suits protect astronauts from harmful sunlight, which is much stronger in space than on Earth. Tubes of cooled water run through the suits to keep astronauts from getting too hot.

A machine makes oxygen for the astronauts to breathe.

Astronauts travel to and from the ISS in spacecraft such as the SpaceX Dragon.

Astronauts feel weightless on the ISS. Everything floats around the space station, so items must be strapped down!

Water would just float away, so there are no showers. Everyone washes with a damp cloth and soap.

Dry food is stored in pouches, and hot water is added at mealtimes.

EXPLORING DEEP SPACE

Space is an enormous place, and traveling across the solar system takes a long time. A one-way trip to Neptune would take 12 years! Instead of risking human lives on these lengthy journeys, machines are sent instead.

VOYAGER

The space probes *Voyager 1* and *Voyager 2* left Earth's orbit in 1977. They are now exploring interstellar space—the area between the stars. The twin probes have explored Jupiter, Saturn, Uranus, Neptune, and 48 moons.

The Voyager probes carry a message in case they should meet any other living thing that might want to learn about life on Earth.

NEW HORIZONS

New Horizons was the first spacecraft to explore Pluto and its moons. It discovered a heart-shaped area of ice on Pluto.

After Pluto, *New Horizons* went on to explore the Kuiper Belt.

ARTEMIS

The Artemis missions will return humans to the moon. The plan is to build a base camp on the moon where astronauts will be able to live and work.

Using the base camp, scientists will be able to explore and investigate more and for longer periods of time.

JUNO

In 2011, the *Juno* spacecraft started its five-year journey to begin orbiting Jupiter. It has helped scientists understand how Jupiter formed and is now exploring its moons.

By early 2023, *Juno* had orbited Jupiter 50 times.

CASSINI-HUYGENS

Cassini spent 20 years in space, studying Saturn and its rings. Its companion module, *Huygens*, landed on Titan, one of Saturn's moons. It discovered that Titan has many ingredients needed to support life—all except warmth.

Cassini traveled 4.9 billion miles/7.9 billion kilometers, orbited Saturn 294 times, and discovered six moons.

PARKER SOLAR PROBE

The Parker Solar Probe flies through space at about 430,000 miles/ 700,000 kilometers per hour. It has gotten closer to the sun than any other probe and has collected information about our star.

The Parker Solar Probe is the fastest object ever made.

LIFE IN OUTER SPACE

The universe is so huge that scientists believe there may be other planets and moons in the solar system and beyond where life could exist.

Earth is called the Goldilocks planet because it is "just right" for supporting life. It has air, liquid water, and the chemicals needed for living things to survive. Space missions are searching for more Goldilocks planets.

Exoplanets are planets outside the solar system. They are a good place to start looking for life in outer space. Space telescopes, such as the James Webb Space Telescope, have found thousands of them so far. If they have atmospheres and liquid water, exoplanets may have living things on them.

No alien life-forms have been discovered yet.

The James Webb Space Telescope is the most powerful telescope ever sent into space.

It uses a type of light called infrared to learn about the history of the universe.

TESS is searching for Earth-like exoplanets.

The James Webb Space Telescope has a metal mirror the size of a tennis court, with 18 panels. Its instruments can look at hundreds of objects at once.

The Roman Space Telescope will be searching for exoplanets by looking closely within the Milky Way and by using its wide field of view to survey a billion galaxies at once.

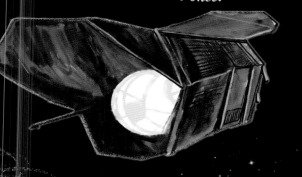

HD 189733b

Winds on a giant exoplanet called HD 189733b travel up to 5,400 miles/ 8,700 kilometers per hour and may bring a sideways rain of glass shards.

Scientists have theorized that exoplanet 55 Cancri e may have carbon in diamond form in its interior.

Exoplanet 55 Cancri e is a super-Earth: a rocky planet between the size of Earth and Neptune.

55 CANCRI E

Enceladus is one of Saturn's moons. It has an icy surface but is warmer underneath, with watery oceans. It's possible that living things are in those oceans.

ENCELADUS

Enceladus is the 19th-largest moon in the solar system.

SPACE WORDS

ASTEROID
A small, rocky object in space

ASTRONAUT
A person who travels in space

ASTRONOMER
A person who studies space

ASTRONOMY
The study of space

ATMOSPHERE
The layer of gases that surrounds
a planet or moon

BILLION
1,000,000,000

BLACK HOLE
An area in space where gravity is so strong
that anything close to it cannot escape

COMET
An object in space that is made of rock, dust,
and icy gases. A comet has a tail, which
points away from the sun.

COMMAND MODULE
The control section of a spacecraft

CONSTELLATION
One of 88 groups of stars that
make an imaginary picture

CONTINENT
One of Earth's main
large areas of land

DORMANT
In a state of inactivity for a long time

DWARF PLANET
An object that orbits the sun but
is smaller than a planet

EQUATOR
An invisible line that circles Earth halfway
between the North and South Poles

GALAXY
A huge group of stars, gas, and dust
that are all held together by gravity

GAS GIANT
A large planet made mostly of
hydrogen, helium, and other gases

GRAVITY
A force that pulls things toward the
center of a planet or other object in
space, such as a moon or sun

HEMISPHERE
Half of a sphere

HORIZON
The line we see in the distance
where land appears to meet the sky

LIGHT-YEAR
The distance that light travels in
one year in the vacuum of space

LUNAR MODULE
The part of a spacecraft that
lands on the moon

SHOOTING STAR SEARCH

Shooting stars, or meteors, are small rocks or specks of dust from space. Did you find all the blue shooting stars in this book? There isn't one on pages 18–19.

METEOR / METEORITE
A meteor is a rocky object that flies through Earth's atmosphere, burning as it travels. If it reaches Earth's surface, it is called a meteorite.

MILLION
1,000,000

MOON
A natural object that orbits a planet

NEBULA
A cloud of gas and dust in space

NEUTRON STAR
A type of star that forms after a supernova explosion

OBSERVATORY
A place where equipment, such as telescopes, is kept for studying space

ORBIT
The path that something follows around a planet or star

PARTICLES
Very small objects

PAYLOAD
The objects or people carried by a spacecraft

PLANET
A large, round object in space that orbits a star

SATELLITE
An artificial object that orbits a planet

SHOOTING STAR
Another name for a meteor as it burns in Earth's atmosphere

SOLAR SYSTEM
A star and the objects, such as planets, that orbit it

STAR
A bright ball of gases in space. The sun is a star.

SUN
The star at the center of our solar system

SUPERNOVA
A star that is exploding and becomes much brighter

TRILLION
1,000,000,000,000

ULTRAVIOLET RADIATION
A type of energy that exists in sunlight

UNIVERSE
Space and everything in it

X-RAY RADIATION
A type of energy that passes through many materials that light cannot pass through

FIRST US EDITION 2024
FIRST PUBLISHED BY TEMPLAR BOOKS, AN IMPRINT OF BONNIER BOOKS UK, 2023

LIBRARY OF CONGRESS CATALOG CARD NUMBER PENDING
ISBN 978-1-5362-3834-1

24 25 26 27 28 29 LEO 10 9 8 7 6 5 4 3 2 1

PRINTED IN HESHAN, GUANGDONG, CHINA

THIS BOOK WAS TYPESET IN GARDEN GROWN AND ESTILO TEXT.
THE ILLUSTRATIONS WERE DONE IN MIXED MEDIA.

ASTRONOMY EXPERTISE PROVIDED BY JAKE FOSTER OF THE ROYAL OBSERVATORY GREENWICH,
PART OF ROYAL MUSEUMS GREENWICH

BIG PICTURE PRESS
AN IMPRINT OF
CANDLEWICK PRESS
99 DOVER STREET
SOMERVILLE, MASSACHUSETTS 02144

WWW.CANDLEWICK.COM